On The One Hand...

The Economist's Joke Book

Economic Futurist Jeff Thredgold

Thredgold Economic Associates
A professional speaking and economic consulting company
www.thredgold.com

ISBN 0-9707226-1-3

Printed and Bound by
Carr Printing Co., Inc., Bountiful, UT
Cover Design by Aaron Jasinski
Layout by L. Dien Parker
Editorial Assistance by Rick Evans

INTRODUCTION

Think about it. What profession is the subject of more jokes and humor than that of being an economist.

...OK, other than lawyers—who clearly deserve the abuse.

Economics is known as "the dismal science." It can be a bit intimidating, boring, frustrating, and confusing in the hands of an amateur. It gets even worse in the hands of a professional.

As a friend of mine suggests (and he's a lawyer!), it's high time economics is given the respect and status it deserves alongside all the other occult sciences.

The following jokes are largely from a list I have compiled over my 26 years in the profession. Names, dates, and raw language have been changed to protect the innocent.

Also included are some of the less insightful quotes of the past few generations. While these people were not economists, they showed real potential.

As an economic futurist and professional speaker, I have found that using humor when speaking and writing makes economics more tolerable. Having some fun with the dismal science is what this book is all about. I hope you enjoy it...and pass it along to a friend.

About the Cover

President Harry S. Truman once said he wanted an economist who was one-handed. Why? Because his economic advisors would typically give him economic advice stating, "On the one hand....And on the other...."

"I'm thinking of leaving my husband," complained the economist's wife to a friend.

"All he ever does is stand at the end of the bed and tell me how good things are going to be."

I asked an economist for her phone number.

...She gave me an estimate.

A philosopher, a biologist, an architect, and an economist were arguing about what God's first profession might have been.

The philosopher said, "Well, first and foremost, God was a philosopher, because he created the principles by which people are to live."

"Ridiculous!" said the biologist. "Before that, God created woman and man and all living things. So clearly, he was a biologist."

"Wrong," said the architect. "Before that, he created the heavens and the earth. Before the earth, there was only confusion and chaos!"

"Well," laughed the economist, "And where do you think the chaos came from?"

What do economists use for birth control?

Their personalities.

"Having a little inflation is like being a little pregnant..."

—Dian Cohen

A guy walks into a bar and shouts loudly, "Economists are jerks!"

A man sitting at the bar jumps up and shouts back, "I greatly resent that statement!"

The first guy asks, "Why. Are you an economist?"

The man quickly responds, "No! I'm a jerk."

Q: Why do economists provide estimates of inflation to the nearest tenth of a percent?

A: To prove they have a sense of humor.

"An economist is an expert who will know tomorrow why the things they predicted yesterday didn't happen today."

—Laurence J. Peter

A man was sent to Hell for his sins. As he was being processed, he passed a room where an economist he knew was having an intimate conversation with a beautiful woman.

"What a crummy deal!" The man complained. "I have to burn for all eternity and that economist spends it with that gorgeous woman."

An escorting demon jabs the man with his pitchfork and shouts, "Who are you to question that woman's punishment?"

Two economists meet on the street. One inquires of the other, "How's your husband?"

The other responds, "Relative to what?"

Top 10 Reasons to Study Economics

1. Economists are armed and dangerous: "Watch out for our invisible hands."

2. Economists can supply it on demand.

3. You can talk about money without ever having to make any.

4. You get to say "trickle down" with a straight face.

5. Mick Jagger and Arnold Schwarzenegger both studied economics, and look how they turned out.

6. When you are in the unemployment line, at least you will know why you're there.

7. If you rearrange the letters in "ECONOMICS" you get "COMIC NOSE."

8. Although ethics teaches that virtue is its own reward, in economics we get taught that reward is its own virtue.

9. When you get drunk, you can tell everyone that you are just researching the law of diminishing marginal utility.

10. Economists do it with models.

Economics is the only field in which two people can receive a Nobel Prize for saying exactly the opposite thing.

A woman approached an economist who was having a night-cap in a sleazy bar. She stated, "I will do ANYTHING you want for $100." He had her paint his condo.

An economist was standing on the shore of a large lake, surf casting. It was the middle of winter and the lake was completely frozen over. This didn't seem to bother the economist, who stood there patiently casting his lure out across the ice, slowly reeling it in again, and then repeating the process.

A mathematical economist came sailing by on an ice boat and pulled to the shore beside the surf fishing economist to scoff. "You'll never catch any fish that way," said the mathematical economist. "Jump on my ice boat and we'll go trawling."

"Everything that can be invented has been invented."

—Charles H. Duell, Commissioner, U.S. Office of Patents, 1899

Economists are people who don't know what they're talking about—and make you feel that it's your fault.

A mother and daughter were walking through a cemetery and passed by a headstone inscribed, "Here lies a good economist and an honest man."

The little girl read the headstone, looked up at her mother, and asked "Mommy, why did they bury two people here?"

Christopher Columbus was perhaps the first economist.

When he left to discover America, he didn't know where he was going.

When he got there, he didn't know where he was.

When he returned, he didn't know where he had been.

And it was all done on a government grant.

Q: What's the difference between an economist and a befuddled old man with Alzheimer's?

A: The economist is the one with the calculator.

Two adventurers, George and Harry, set out in a hot air balloon to cross the Continent. After 37 hours in the air, George says, “Harry, we better lose some altitude so we can see where we are.”

Harry lets out some of the hot air in the balloon, and they descend to below the cloud cover. George says, “I still can’t tell where we are. Let’s ask that woman on the ground.”

Harry yells down to the woman, “Hey, could you tell us where we are?” The woman on the ground yells back, “You’re in a balloon, 100 feet in the air.”

George turns to Harry and says, “That woman must be an economist.” Harry says, “How can you tell?” George says, “Because the answer she gave us is 100% accurate and totally useless.”

Three economists went out hunting and came across a large deer.

The first economist fired, but missed by a yard to the left.

The second economist fired, but also missed, by a yard to the right.

The third economist didn't fire, but shouted in triumph, "We got it! We got it!"

Economics is the painful elaboration of the obvious.

There are three kinds of economists—those who can count, and those who can't.

"We have two classes of forecasters:

Those who don't know...

And those who don't know they don't know."

—John Kenneth Galbraith
(a well-known economist)

Two economists were walking down the street when they noticed two men yelling across the street at each other from their apartment windows. "Of course they will never come to an agreement," stated the first economist.

"And why is that," inquired her companion. "Why, of course, because they are arguing from different premises."

"If all economists were laid end to end they would not reach a conclusion."
—George Bernard Shaw

A civil engineer, a chemist, and an economist are traveling in the countryside. Weary, they stop at a small country inn. "I only have two rooms, so one of you will have to sleep in the barn," the innkeeper says. The civil engineer volunteers to sleep in the barn, goes outside, and the others go to bed.

In a short time, they're awakened by a knock. It's the engineer, who says, "There's a cow in that barn. I'm a Hindu, and it would offend my beliefs to sleep next to a sacred animal."

The chemist says that's OK, she will sleep in the barn. The others go back to bed, but soon are awakened by another knock. It's the chemist, who says, "There's a pig in that barn.

I'm Jewish, and cannot sleep next to an unclean animal."

So the economist goes to the barn. It's getting late. The others are very tired and soon fall asleep. But they are awakened by an even louder knocking sound. They open the door and are surprised by what they see: the cow and the pig!

A group of economists was climbing in the Alps. After several hours they became hopelessly lost.

One of them studied the map for some time, turning it up and down, sighting on distant landmarks, consulting his compass, and the sun's location. Finally, he said, "OK, see that big mountain over there?"

"Yes," answered the others eagerly. "Well, according to the map, we're standing on top of it."

Two female friends were taking an Economics class from a very boring professor. They did well on the quizzes, assignments, and tests, and felt they had A's going into the final exam.

They decided to go partying the weekend before the early Monday morning exam. However, with hangovers in abundance, they slept through the final. On Monday afternoon, they contacted the professor and explained to her that they had been out of town on Sunday and had a flat tire.

They asked to take the final the following morning. The professor agreed.

They studied that night and approached the delayed final exam with confidence. The professor placed the two women in separate rooms, handed each a test booklet, and told them to begin.

They looked at the first question, worth five points, and each answered it with ease. This was going to be easy!

They then turned the page and found the following: (95 points) Which tire?

Q: What do you get when you cross a pilgrim with a Democrat?

A: A God-fearing tax collector who gives thanks for what other people have.

"But what...is it good for?"
—Engineer at the Advanced Computing Systems Division of IBM, 1968, commenting on the microchip

Did you hear of the economist who dove into her swimming pool and broke her neck?

She forgot to "seasonally adjust" her pool.

A wealthy labor economist had an urge to have grandchildren. He had two daughters and two sons and none of them had gratified his desire for a grandchild.

At the annual family gathering on Thanksgiving Day, he chided them gently to bless his old age with their progeny. "But I haven't given up hope," he said. "Yesterday, I went to the bank and set up a $1,000,000 trust fund to be given to the first grandchild that I have."

"Now we will all bow our heads while I say a prayer of thanks." When he looked up, he and his wife were the only ones at the table.

Dear Abby,

I have two brothers. One is an economist and the other was sent to the electric chair.

I have two sisters. One is a well-known prostitute and the other is the leader of an organization planning to overthrow the government.

My mother died in an insane asylum. My father has been peddling drugs since I was a child.

I just met a wonderful woman who will soon be released from prison for the ax murder of her parents. We are very much in love and plan to marry.

My problem? Should I tell her about my brother who is an economist?

An "acceptable" level of unemployment means that the government economist to whom it is acceptable still has a job.

When Albert Einstein passed away, St. Peter placed him in a room with three other people. A woman rushed up to Einstein and stated what a pleasure it was to meet him. She also stated, "By the way, my IQ is 165." "Wonderful," exclaimed Einstein. "We can discuss my theory of relativity."

A gentleman approached Einstein and stated that his IQ was 145. "Great!" said Einstein. "I look forward to discussing quantum physics with you for hours on end."

Another gentleman was cowering in the corner. Einstein approached him with his outstretched hand and asked his IQ. "Well, my IQ is only 75," stated the man quietly. "That's great as well, my friend," stated Einstein. "Where do you think interest rates are headed?"

An elderly economics professor stands near the shallow end of the campus swimming pool. A female student stands near the deep end taking pictures. She suddenly drops the camera into the pool.

She then motions for the professor to come to her. He goes to her, and she asks him to retrieve the camera. He agrees, dives in, and retrieves it.

Upon returning, he says to her, "Why did you ask me to retrieve the camera when there were many younger and more athletic men closer to you?" She replied, "Professor, I'm in your Economics 101 class. I don't know anyone who can go down deeper, stay down longer, and come up any dryer than you."

Q: How many Wall Street economists does it take to screw in a light bulb?

A: Just one—He holds the light bulb and the whole earth revolves around him.

"There are two things you are better off not watching in the making: sausages and econometric estimates."

—Edward Leamer

A recession is when your neighbor has lost her job.

A depression is when you lose yours.

A grade school teacher was asking students what their parents did for a living. "Kacey, you be first. What does your mother do all day?"

Kacey stood up and proudly said, "She's a professional violinist." "That's wonderful. How about you, Amy?"

Amy shyly stood up, scuffed her feet and said, "My father is a mailman."

"Thank you, Amy" said the teacher. "What does your father do, Chris?"

Chris proudly stood up and announced, "My daddy plays piano in a whorehouse."

The teacher was aghast and went to Chris's house and rang the bell. Chris's father answered the door.

The teacher explained what his son had said and demanded an explanation. Chris's dad said, "I'm actually an economist. But, how can I explain a thing like that to a seven-year-old?"

Economics is like red wine—you shouldn't smell it, but drink it.

But if you drink too much on one occasion, there is a risk of dizziness.

One day a man walked into the main library of a major research university. He stopped at the reference desk and asked the librarian if she had any current books about the economy. She answered that she did and led the man to the reference shelves where the economics books were located.

To the surprise of both the librarian and the man, all of the books were being used. "That's OK," the man said. "I'll just go to another library. You see, I'm a very busy man, and I set this weekend aside for studying about the economy."

The librarian said she understood and gave the man directions to the nearest research library. But her interest piqued, she asked, "Why are you so urgent to study economics and the economy?"

The man replied, "I'm an economist. I've been teaching at this university for the past ten years. I'm attending a business meeting on Monday, and I figure the economy might have changed in the past ten years."

"We don't like their sound, and guitar music is on the way out."

—Decca Recording Company
in rejecting the Beatles, 1962

An economist is someone who knows the price of everything and the value of nothing.

One day a woman went for a walk in her neighborhood and came across a boy with some puppies. "Would you like a puppy? They aren't ready for new homes quite yet, but they will be in a few weeks!"

"Oh, they're adorable," the lady said. "What kind of dogs are they?" "These are economists."

"OK. I'll tell my husband." So she went home and told her husband. He was very interested in seeing the puppies.

About a week later, he came across the lad. The puppies were very active. "Hey, Mister. Want a puppy?" "I think my wife spoke with you last week," stated the man. "What kind of dogs are these?"

"Oh. These are decision analysts," stated the boy proudly. "I thought you said last week that they were economists," said the man.

"Well yes...But now their eyes are open."

ECONOMISTS do it cyclically

American President George W. Bush and Russian President Vladimir Putin are taking a break from a long summit. Putin says to Bush, George, I have a big problem I don't know what to do about. I have 100 body-guards and one of them is a traitor. I don't know which one."

"I know the problem, Vladimir. I'm stuck with a dozen economists I have to listen to all the time before I make any policy decision, and only one tells the truth...But it's never the same one."

A veteran economist and a rookie economist are walking down the road. They come across a spoiled apple lying on the asphalt. Says the veteran economist, "If you eat it, I'll give you $20,000!"

The rookie economist runs his optimization model and figures out he's better off eating it. He does so and collects the money.

Continuing along the same road, they almost step on a spoiled banana. The rookie economist states, "Now, if YOU eat that banana, I'll give YOU $20,000." After evaluating the proposal, the veteran economist eats the spoiled fruit, and soon collects the money.

As they continue walking, the rookie economist starts thinking and states, "Listen. We both have the same amount of money we had before, but we both ate spoiled fruit. I don't see us being better off."

States the veteran economist, "Well that's true, but you overlook the fact that we've just been involved in $40,000 of trade."

"A study of economics usually reveals that the best time to buy anything was last year."

—Marty Allen

What is an economist's dream date?

A loaf of bread, a jug of wine, and you beside me watching Louis Rukeyser.

An economist was crossing a road one day when a frog called out to him and said, "If you kiss me, I'll turn into a beautiful princess." He bent over, picked up the frog, and put it in his pocket. The frog spoke up again and said, "If you kiss me and turn me back into a beautiful princess, I will stay with you for one week."

The economist took the frog out of his pocket, smiled at it, and returned it to his pocket. The frog then cried out, "If you kiss me and turn me back into a princess, I'll stay with you for a week, and do ANYTHING you want." Again the economist took the frog out, smiled at it and put it back into his pocket.

Finally, the frog asked, "What's the matter with you? I've told you I'm a beautiful princess, and that I'll stay with you for a week, and do anything you want. Why won't you kiss me?"

The man said, "Look, I'm an economist. I don't have time for a girlfriend...But a talking frog is cool."

Two strangers, a man and a woman, meet in a café. The man soon asks, "My Dear, would you go to bed with me for a million dollars?" "Well, yes, I guess I would."

"How about $100?" "$100? What kind of person do you think I am?"

"My Dear, we have already established that. We are now merely negotiating the price!"

A woman hears from her doctor that she has only half a year to live. The doctor advises her to marry an economist.

The woman asks, "Will this cure my illness?" The doctor answers, "No. But the six months will seem like a lifetime."

PURE POLITICS

Socialism:

You have two cows. The State takes one and gives it to someone else.

Communism:

You have two cows. The State takes both of them and gives you milk.

Fascism:

You have two cows. The State takes both of them and sells you milk.

Dictatorship:

You have two cows. The government takes both and shoots you.

Environmentalism:

You have two cows. The government bans you from milking or selling them.

Totalitarianism:

You have two cows. The government takes them and denies they ever existed. Milk is banned.

Political Correctness:

You are associated with (the concept of "ownership" is a symbol of the phallo-centric, war-mongering, intolerant past) two different-aged (but no less valuable to society) bovines of non-specified gender.

Counter Culture:

"Wow, dude, there's like...these two cows, man. You got to have some of this milk. Far out!"

Capitalism:

You have two cows. You sell one and buy a bull.

It's not easy being an economist.

How would you like to go through life pretending you knew what M1 was all about?

Q: Why did God create economists?

A: To make astrologers look good.

"An economist is someone who sees something working in practice and asks whether it would work in principle."

—Stephen Goldfield

Q: How many economists does it take to change a light bulb?

A: Eight. One to screw it in and seven to hold everything else constant.

A man walking along a road in the countryside comes across a shepherd and a huge flock of sheep. He tells the shepherd, "I will bet you $100 against one of your sheep that I can tell you the exact number in this flock."

The shepherd thinks it over. It's a large flock, so he accepts the bet. "There are 973 sheep," says the man. The shepherd is astonished, because that is exactly right. "OK, I'm a man of my word, take one." The man picks one up and begins to walk away.

"Wait," cries the shepherd. "Let me have a chance to get even. Double or nothing that I can guess your exact occupation." The man agrees.

"You are an economist for a government think tank," says the shepherd. "Amazing!" responds the man. "You are exactly right! But tell me, how did you deduce that?"

"Well," says the shepherd, "Put down my dog and I'll tell you."

This tale is said to be told by John Kenneth Galbraith (a famous economist) regarding himself. As a boy, he lived on a farm in Canada. On the adjoining farm lived a girl he was fond of.

One day, as they sat together on the top rail of the cattle pen, they watched a bull servicing a cow. Galbraith turned to the girl, with what he hoped was a suggestive look, saying, "That looks like it would be fun."

She replied, "Well...It's your cow."

Back during the Solidarity days, the following joke was being told in Poland:

A man goes into the Bank of Gdansk to make a deposit. Since he has never kept money in a bank before, he is a little nervous.

"What happens if the Bank of Gdansk should fail?" he asks. "Well, in that case your money would be insured by the Bank of Warsaw."

"But, what if the Bank of Warsaw fails?" "Well, there'd be no problem, because the Bank of Warsaw is insured by the National Bank of Poland."

"And if the National Bank of Poland fails?" "Then your money would be insured by the Bank of Moscow."

"And what if the Bank of Moscow fails?" "Then your money would be insured by the Great Bank of the Soviet Union."

"And if that bank fails?" "Well, in that case, you'd lose all your money."

"But, wouldn't it be worth it?"

Economists have forecast 9 out of the last 5 recessions.

"Someone once said about economists that they use economic data the way a drunkard uses a lamppost...For support rather than illumination."

"Or as Disraeli put it, there are three kinds of lies: lies, damn lies, and statistics."

—Paul Krugman (a well-known economist)

Two economists sit down to play chess.

They study the board for 24 hours and declare a stalemate.

"Economic statistics are like a bikini. What they reveal is important... what they conceal is vital."

—Sir Frank Holmes

"In explaining why she felt our relationship had problems, a former girlfriend (an English teacher) told me that the problem was that I was so...so...reasonable."

—David Colander

Economic forecasting is like trying to drive a car blindfolded and following directions given by a person who is looking out of the back window.

Borrowing an idea from one source is called plagiarism.

Borrowing from many sources is called research.

Economists are people who are too smart for their own good and not smart enough for anyone else's.

An Economics Limerick...

Folks came from afar just to see
Two economists who'd agreed to
agree.
While the event did take place,
It proved a disgrace.
They agreed one plus one adds to
three.

—Robley E. George

A joke on the streets of Moscow these days goes this way:

"Everything the Communists told us about communism was a complete and utter lie."

"Unfortunately, everything they told us about Capitalism turned out to be true."

"I think there is a world market for maybe five computers."

—Thomas Watson,
Chairman of IBM, 1943

An economist is someone who gets rich explaining to others why they are poor.

A student named Michelle was taking a class taught by Milton Friedman at the University of Chicago. After a late night studying, she fell asleep in class.

This sent Friedman into a little tizzy and he came over and pounded on the table, demanding an answer to a question he had just posed to the class. Michelle, now awake, said "I'm sorry, Professor. I missed the question, but the answer is increase the money supply."

"The wireless music box has no imaginable commercial value. Who would pay for a message sent to nobody in particular?"

—David Sarnoff's associates in response to his urgings for investment in the radio in the 1920s

A traveler wandering on an island inhabited entirely by cannibals comes upon a butcher shop. This shop specialized in human brains, separated according to source.

The sign in the shop read:

Artists' Brains	$9/lb
Philosophers' Brains	$12/lb
Scientists' Brains	$15/lb
Economists' Brains	$79/lb

Upon reading the sign, the traveler notes, "My those economists' brains must be popular!" To which the butcher replies, "Are you kidding! Do you have any idea how many economists it takes to get a pound of brains?"

"Who the hell wants to hear actors talk?"

—H.M. Warner, Warner Brothers, 1927

In Canada there is a small radical group that refuses to speak English and no one can understand them.

They are called separatists.

In this country, we have the same kind of group.

They are called economists.

—*Nation's Business*

Achieving free trade is like getting to heaven.

Everyone wants to get there, but not too soon.

"I'd rather be vaguely right than precisely wrong."

—John Maynard Keynes,
father of Keynesian economics

Three leading economists took a small plane to the wilderness in northern Canada to hunt moose over the weekend. The last thing the pilot said was, "Remember, this is a very small plane. You will only be able to bring ONE moose back."

But of course, they each shot one. On Sunday, they talked the pilot into letting them bring all three moose onboard.

Just after takeoff, the plane stalled and crashed. In the wreckage, one of the economists regained consciousness, looked around and said, "Where the hell are we."

Says another, "Oh, about a hundred yards East of the place where we crashed last year."

On the first day, God created the sun. The Devil countered and created sunburn.

On the second day, God created sex. In response, the Devil created marriage.

On the third day, God created an economist. This was a tough one for the Devil, but in the end, and after a lot of thought, he created a second economist!

An economist returns to visit her old school. She's interested in the current exam questions and asks her old professor to show her some.

To her surprise, they are exactly the same ones that she had answered 10 years ago! When she asked the professor about this, the professor answered, "The questions are always the same. Only the answers change!"

"This 'telephone' has too many shortcomings to be seriously considered as a means of communication. The device is inherently of no value to us."

—Western Union internal memo, 1876

Q: What is a recent economics graduate's usual question in their first job?

A: Would you like fries with your burger?

An economist was asked about the meaning of life.

He replied: It depends on the parameter values.

Three guys decide to play a round of golf: a priest, a psychologist, and an economist. They get behind a very slow twosome, who, despite having caddies, are taking all day to line up their shots and then four-putting every green. By the 8th hole, the three men are complaining loudly about the slow play ahead and swearing up a storm.

The priest says, "Holy Mary, I pray that they should take some lessons before they play again." The psychologist says, "I swear there are people that like to play golf slowly." The economist says, "I really didn't expect to spend this much time playing a round of golf."

By the 9th hole, they have had it with slow play. The psychologist goes up to a caddie and demands that they be allowed to play through. A caddie says that would be fine, and explains that the two golfers are blind, and that both are retired fire-men who lost their eyesight saving people in a fire. This explains their slow play, states the caddie. "Would you please not swear and complain so loudly."

The priest is mortified, saying, "Here I am, a man of the cloth and I've been swearing at the slow play of two blind men." The psychologist is also mortified, saying, "Here I am a man trained to help others with their problems, and I've also been complaining about the slow play of two blind men."

The economist ponders the situation. He goes back to the caddies and states, "Listen, the next time they play, could it be at night?"

Economics is extremely useful as a form of employment for economists.

An economist is someone who didn't have enough personality to become an accountant.

Q: What does it take to be a good economist?

A: An unshakable grasp of the obvious!

"I'm just glad it'll be Clark Gable who's falling on his face and not Gary Cooper."

—Gary Cooper
on his decision not to take the
leading role in "Gone With The Wind"

"There is no reason anyone would want a computer in their home."

—Ken Olson, President, Chairman and founder of Digital Equipment Corp., 1977

The mathematician's child and the economist's child were in the third grade together. The teacher asked, "If one man with one shovel can dig a ditch in ten days, how long would it take ten men with ten shovels to dig the same ditch?" Both children raised their hands.

The teacher said to the mathematician's child, "Shawn, how long?" Little Shawn answered, "One day, teacher."

The teacher looked at the economist's child and said, "John Maynard, is that right?"

Little John Maynard said, Teacher, it all depends."

A physicist, a chemist, and an economist are stranded on an island, with nothing to eat. A can of soup washes ashore.

The physicist says, "Let's smash the can open with a rock."

The chemist says, "Let's build a fire and heat the can first."

The economist says, "Lets assume that we have a can opener..."

—Paul Samuelson
(a well-known economist)

The First Law of Economics:

For every economist, there exists an equal and opposite economist.

The Second Law of Economics:

They're both wrong.

A central bank economist walks into a pizzeria to order a pizza. When the pizza is done, she goes up to the counter to get it.

There a clerk asks her, "Should I cut it into six pieces or eight pieces?" The central banker replies, "I'm feeling rather hungry right now."

"You'd better cut it into eight pieces."

An economist is someone who knows 100 ways to make love...But doesn't know any women/men.

"640K ought to be enough for anybody."

—Bill Gates, 1981

There is a story about the last May Day parade in the Soviet Union. After the tanks and the troops and the planes and the missiles rolled by, there came ten people dressed in black.

"Are they spies?" Asked the Russian Premier?

"They are economists," replies the KGB director. "Imagine the havoc they will wreak when we set them loose on the Americans."

A guy walks into a Washington D.C. curio shop. While browsing, he comes across an exquisite brass rat.

"What a great gag gift" he thinks to himself. After dickering with the shopkeeper over the price, the man purchases the rat and leaves.

As he's walking down the street, he hears scurrying noises behind him. Stopping and looking around, he sees hundreds, then thousands of rats pouring out of the alleys and stairwells into the street behind him. In a panic, he runs down the street with the rats not far behind.

The street ends at a pier. He runs to the end of the pier and heaves the brass rat into the Potomac River. All of the rats scurry past him into the river, where they drown.

After breathing a sigh of relief and wiping his brow, the man heads back to the curio shop, finds the shopkeeper, and asks, "Do you have any brass economists?"

If an economist and an IRS agent were both drowning and you could only save one of them...would you go to lunch or read the paper?

"I have traveled the length and breadth of this country and talked with the best people, and I can assure you that data processing is a fad that won't last out the year."

—The editor in charge of business books for Prentice Hall, 1957

TEN THINGS TO DO WITH A GRADUATE ECONOMICS TEXTBOOK

1. Press pretty flowers.

2. Press pretty insects.

3. Use it as a paperweight on your already cluttered desk.

4. Leave out in obvious places to impress uninformed friends.

5. Mail to the White House as an intimidation tactic.

6. Tear it into pieces for cat litter.

7. Just throw the damn thing away.

8. Leave out for the rain and other forces of nature to reckon with.

9. Read it (ha ha), and weep.

10. Get a refund from the bookstore so you can buy the weekend's beer supply.

Economists don't answer questions others ask because they know the answer.

They answer because they are asked.

ECONOMISTS do it with crystal balls.

Why do economists carry their diplomas on their dashboards?

So they can park in the handicapped parking.

"Shall I tell you the opinion of a famous economist on jealousy? Jealousy is just the fact of being deprived...Nothing more."

—Henry Becque

How can you tell when an economist is wrong?

Their lips are moving.

Another school teacher asked her students what their parents did for a living. “Kennadie, you be first. What does your mother do all day?”

Kennadie stood up and proudly said, “She’s an operating room nurse.” “That’s wonderful. How about you, Drew?”

Drew shyly stood up, scuffed his feet and said, “My father is a plumber.”

“Thank you Drew,” said the teacher. “What does your father do, Taylor?”

Taylor proudly stood up and announced, “Nothing. He’s an economist.”

“Heavier-than-air flying machines are impossible.”

—Lord Kelvin,

President, Royal Society, 1895

An East Coast economic consultant died and went to heaven (No, that's not the joke). There were thousands of people ahead of him in line to see St. Peter.

To his surprise, St. Peter left his desk at the gate and came down the long line to where the economist was and greeted him warmly.

St. Peter took the economist up to the front of the line, and placed him into a comfortable chair by his desk. The economist said, "I like all this attention, but what makes ME so special?"

St. Peter replied, "Well, I've added up all the hours for which you billed your consulting clients, and by my calculation you're 151 years old!"

For three years, the young economics professor took his vacations at a country inn. He had an affair with the innkeeper's daughter. Looking forward to an exciting few days, he dragged his suitcase up the stairs of the inn, then stopped short.

There sat his lover with an infant on her lap! "Why didn't you write when you learned you were pregnant?" he cried. "I would have rushed up here, we could have gotten married, and the child would have my name!"

"Well," she said, "when my folks found out about my condition, we sat up all night talkin' and talkin' and we finally decided it would be better to have a bastard in the family than an economist."

"Computers in the future may weigh no more than 1.5 tons."

—Popular Mechanics, forecasting the relentless march of science, 1949

What's the difference between mathematics and economics?

Mathematics is incomprehensible. Economics just doesn't make any sense.

A Wall Street economist had a summer house in the Maine woods. Each summer he'd invite a different friend to spend a week or two. On one occasion, he invited a friend from the Czech Republic to stay with him. They had a splendid time in the country, rising early and living in the great outdoors.

Early one morning, they went out to pick berries for their morning breakfast. As they went around the berry patch, along came two huge bears. The economist dashed for cover. His friend wasn't so lucky and the male bear reached him and swallowed him whole.

The economist ran back to his car, drove to town as fast as he could, and got the sheriff. The sheriff grabbed his rifle and dashed back to the berry patch with the economist. Sure enough, both bears were still there.

"He's in THAT one!" cried the economist, pointing to the male. The sheriff looked at the bears, and without batting an eye leveled his gun, took careful aim, and SHOT THE FEMALE.

"Whatd'ya do that for?" cried the economist, "I said he was in the other!" "Yup," said the sheriff, "and would YOU believe an economist who told you the Czech was in the Male?"

Q: How many mainstream economists does it take to change a light bulb?

A: Two. One to assume the existence of a ladder and one to change the bulb.

"Drill for oil? You mean drill into the ground to try and find oil? You're crazy."

—Drillers who Edwin L. Drake tried to enlist to his project to drill for oil in 1859

What helps a pregnant woman identify that her baby will be a future economist?

She has an uncontrollable craving for baloney.

Santa Claus, the tooth fairy, a highly esteemed economist, and an old drunk were walking down the street together when they simultaneously spotted a $100 bill. Who got it?

The old drunk, of course. The other three are mythical creatures.

After saving for years, Lynnette took an extended vacation in Palm Springs. While hanging out at the pool, she noticed an old friend from high school.

She walked over to her friend and became reacquainted. Lynnette also asked what her friend was doing for a living?

"I'm a research economist. But please don't tell my parents. They think I work as a call girl."

A convention of the American Economics Association was taken over by a band of terrorists. More than 200 economists were held hostage.

Until their demands were met, the leader of the terrorists announced that one economist would be released every 20 minutes.

Guess what happens when a Wall Street economist takes Viagra?

He gets taller.

Q: What do you get when you cross the Godfather with an economist?

A: An offer you can't understand.

What's the difference between God and a Wall Street economist?

God doesn't think He's an economist.

"If you put two economists in a room, you get two opinions, unless one of them is Lord Keynes, in which case you get three opinions."

—Winston Churchill

A man entered a New York economic consultant's office and asked what her rates were. "$75.00 for three questions," she replied.

"Isn't that awfully high?" the man asked. "Perhaps," the woman stated.

"And what is your final question?"

DEFINITIONS

Stock:

A magical piece of paper that is worth $33.75 until the moment you buy it. It will then be worth $8.50.

Bond:

What you had with your spouse until you pawned his golf clubs to invest in Priceline.com.

Broker:

The person you trust to help you make major financial decisions. Please note the first five letters of this word spell Broke.

Commission:

The only reliable way to make money in the market, which is why your broker charges you one.

Bear:

What your trading account and wallet will be when you take a flyer on that hot stock tip your golfing buddy gave you.

Bull:

What your broker uses to explain why your mutual funds tanked during the last quarter.

POKING FUN AT YOURSELF

This piece was written a few years ago by Todd Zagorec, a friend and former banking associate at KeyCorp. He now acts (up) as counsel for Huntsman Chemical. Todd has long been miscast in life...he should have been a writer for Leno or Letterman.

This interview is an excerpt from a recent public affairs broadcast. I didn't catch the beginning of the program, so I missed the names. I assume the one with the ouija board was the economist.

Why did you go into your particular field of study?

Lawyer: I found the rules that make society possible to be fascinating.

Economist: I needed a career that would reward exaggeration and guesswork, and this pays better than astrology.

How does one become a lawyer/ economist?

Lawyer: It's important to do well in college, and then study hard for three more years in law school. To get your license, you have to pass a closed-book exam covering all aspects of law, and lasting two or three days. In addition, throughout your career you must satisfy continuing legal education requirements in order to remain a lawyer.

Economist: It all starts with an invitation on a matchbook cover. This is followed by a couple of night classes learning to say things like, "Interest rates will remain stable, assuming they don't rise, fall, or God-forbid...move sideways."

Who are some of your heroes... the role models of your profession?

Lawyer: Abraham Lincoln, Daniel Webster, Clarence Darrow, and Oliver Wendell Holmes.

Economist: Jeanne Dixon, Jimmy the Greek, Willard Scott, and Shirley MacLaine.

If you couldn't be a lawyer/ economist, what would you be?

Lawyer: A writer or a teacher.

Economist: A phrenologist (one who studies bumps on the skull).

Are you involved in any community service?

Lawyer: I'm working on establishing a foundation to provide free legal services to nursing home residents.

Economist: I'm tinkering with a new kind of copper bracelet that's a lot cheaper than the Democrat's desired health care package.

What are your professional goals?

Lawyer: To provide fair and effective representation for my clients.

Economist: To pay off my gambling debts.

Your professions often seem to get more criticism than most. Lawyers are said to be greedy, technical, and unprincipled. Economists are supposedly vague and unscientific. What do you think of that?

Lawyer: I honestly feel the criticism is exaggerated. Lawyers are no worse than the people they represent. Of course there are problems—crowded courts, complicated laws—and I'm hopeful that reform will take place, but that will take a lot of time, imagination, and effort. Difficult problems are never easily solved.

Economist: OK, so economics isn't an exact science like tarot cards, chiropractic, or Kirlian photography, but I think it's every bit as respectable a field as rolfing, channelling, or est. In short, I'm tired of the criticism and think it's high time economics was given the respect and status it deserves alongside all the other occult sciences.

What advice can you give young people who want to succeed?

Lawyer: Your reputation is the most important thing you have.

Economist: Always split aces and eights, and never double down when the dealer shows an ace.

Thank you very much for your time.

Lawyer: You're welcome.

Economist: What about my honorarium?

Speaking Client Comments

"Jeff, very seldom in this business do I have the honor to witness **a perfect rating on a speaker** at one of our meetings. You are one of the few. You were captivating! You are a true professional in every sense of the word."

—Bruce Plummer, VP & Dir. of Education, Tennessee Bankers Association

"Many thanks for providing an informative and entertaining presentation for our users group meeting. **Many attendees tracked me down just to say how much they enjoyed your speech**."

—Michael Miller, President, TIP Technologies, Inc.

"The response to your session was tremendous. (**We even had a few people praise us for choosing you as a speaker!**) I also appreciate your joining us at the social hour following your program. It was refreshing to have a speaker who's willing to take extra time to interact with our membership."

—Mary Roach, Education & Training Dir., Iowa Association of Electric Cooperatives

"You were great! And, yes, economics can be 'entertaining and humorous.' Early feedback shows that yours may have been **one of the best overall sessions we have ever had**."

—M. Lance Miller, CAE, EVP,
Metal Treating Institute

"…your remarks were both highly entertaining and educational. Your insight on the economy, both local and national, was **the perfect presentation for our luncheon session.** I would heartily recommend your presentation to other groups."

—Jill Vicory, Dir., Communications & Education,
Utah Hospitals and Health Systems Association

"**Your 'A' performance received rave reviews.** You did an outstanding job speaking to our members and their customers. **I think the best indicator of my satisfaction with your performance is that I have already hired you to speak at our annual convention in October!**"

—Patricia L. Pines, VP, Education & Convention
Services, American Meat Institute

Who is Jeff Thredgold?

Jeff Thredgold is President of Thredgold Economic Associates, a professional speaking and economic consulting company.

His career includes 23 years with KeyCorp, one of the nation's largest financial services companies, stretching from Maine to Alaska with assets of more than $87 billion, where he served as Senior Vice President and Chief Economist. He currently serves as economic consultant to $23 billion Zions Bancorporation, with banks in eight states, as well as to Zions Bank Capital Markets, one of the nation's 25 primary government bond dealers. Jeff also serves as economic consultant to financial services clients in two other states.

Jeff has appeared dozens of times on CNBC-TV, the nation's business network, as well as numerous appearances on CNN, and is quoted frequently in such publications as *The Wall Street Journal*, USA TODAY, *Investor's Business Daily*, and *Business Week*. He served on the Advisory Committee of the American Bankers Association and the Economic Policy Committee of the U.S. Chamber of Commerce.

Jeff was 1999-2000 President of the National Speakers Association's Utah Chapter, and has spoken more than 1000 times during the past 13 years, traveling more than one million miles in the process. He served as an adjunct professor of finance at the University of Utah for 16 years and formerly served as President of the National Association for Business Economics Utah Chapter.

Jeff received a bachelor's degree in business administration from Weber State University and a master's degree in economics from the University of Utah. In addition, he completed investment banking schools at Southern Methodist University and the University of Illinois.

Economy by Thredgold:

A Common Sense Discussion of the Economy, Money, and Success in the 21st Century

I have been writing an economic and financial newsletter every week for the past 26 years (maybe someday I'll get it right!). This book reflects my view of the way things are—including the good news and the bad news—and the way I think they should be.

I have learned that whether I am speaking or writing about the economy, a little dose of humor goes a long way. Economics—also known as "the dismal science"—gets a bad wrap too frequently as vague and unscientific. To quote a friend, economics should get the respect it deserves alongside the other *occult* sciences.

The 164-page hardcover book is available through my office at 1-888-847-3346 for $22. We will pay shipping, handling and sales tax. *Economy by Thredgold* can also be purchased though Amazon.com.

Our Weekly Update

The *Tea Leaf* is our weekly two-page economic & financial update. Various clients provide it to their customers and employees via their web sites, by hard copy, or as part of their internal publications. Jeff has been writing a weekly update for 26 years.

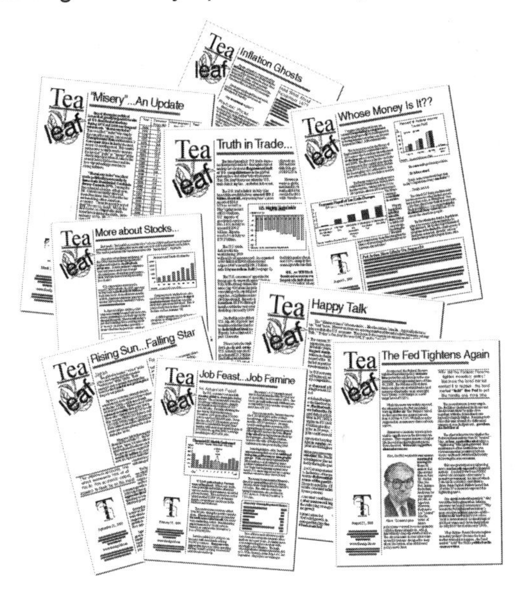

The *Tea Leaf* is available for one year (52 issues) for $79 or two years for $129 (save $29). To subscribe, contact my office at 1-888-847-3346.

A Parent's Letter to My Children in School

I have been writing a weekly update piece under one banner or another for the past 26 years. Seven years ago, I published this letter as "A Father's Letter to My Children in School" and the response was amazing. I had dozens of requests for permission to reprint more than 150,000 copies. Since then, just as children around the country are getting ready to go back to school, I run it again. I hope you enjoy it.

Due to the strong demand for this piece, I have published it as a soft-cover book that is available through my office at (toll-free) 1-888-847-3346 for $3.95, plus $1.25 for shipping/handling. Quantity discounts are available.

The final page says "Love," and then is left blank to be signed by the giver, typically a parent or grandparent.

Jeff Thredgold
Thredgold Economic Associates
136 South Main Street, Suite 417
Salt Lake City, UT 84101
voice (801) 533-9663
fax (801) 533-8273
toll-free 1-888-THREDGOLD
(847-3346)
www.thredgold.com
jeff@thredgold.com